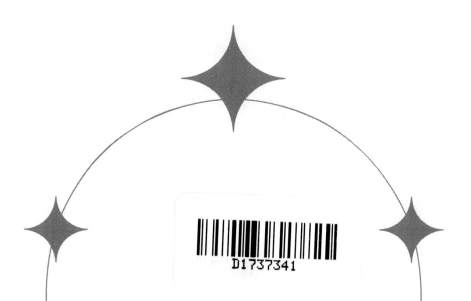

D1737341

this journal belongs to:

_____

created by:
Carolina Salazar (@thecarolinalifestyle) & Sloane Elizabeth (@sloaneelizabeth)

how to use this journal

Welcome to the Manifestation Magnet Journal created by
Carolina Salazar (@thecarolinalifestyle) and Sloane Elizabeth
(@sloaneelizabeth)! We hope you use this magical journal to
co-create the most aligned, high vibe life of your dreams.
Please use this journal every morning to set potent intentions, check
in with your vibrations, and communicate your desires with the
Universe. Below is a description of how to use each prompt – enjoy!

today's word/intention is:

This is your space to get clear on the word, energy, or intention you
want to focus on for the day. Make it something meaningful and
potent that you will remember throughout the day. When life gets
stressful or challenging, use your morning intention to ground you
back in the present moment. Plus: setting an intention is like telling
the universe how you want your day to go.

today I want to feel:

Decide on HOW you want to feel today. This space should
be focused on emotions and the *best case scenario* for
how your day will go.

one thing I can do today to feel that way is:

Part of manifesting is feeling the feelings you want to feel, and feeling
them NOW, perhaps before you even receive the *thing* you think will
get you that feeling. For example, if you want to manifest a romantic
partner that will make you feel loved, you'll want to think of how you
can feel loved TODAY, even without a romantic partner. Brainstorm
one action you can take today to feel the way you said you wanted to
feel in the previous prompt.

I am grateful for :

We love a good gratitude list! Try to get specific and reflect on things that are emotional and meaningful to you. The more grateful and appreciative you feel now for the things you already have, you are saying thanks to the universe for the gifts It's already given you and open up to receive even more abundance!

yesterday's wins:

Like attracts like, so if you want to experience more success, you must first acknowledge and celebrate the success you're already having! And you ARE experiencing success every day – even if they feel like small wins. Acknowledge them all – you deserve to be celebrated!

I trust the Universe to bring in_

Co-creating your dreams requires taking aligned action AND surrendering to the Universe. Surrendering means trusting that your desires are already on their way and the Universe will deliver its part in the most perfect divine timing. This is the space to affirm what you intuitively know the Universe will provide for you and help you with as you manifest your dreams!

today's to-do list:

Stay accountable and grounded in your most important tasks for the day with an aligned to-do list! And remember – these are things that you *get* to do!

date: *2/22/2022*

today's word/intention is...

MAGNETIC!

today I want to feel...
Happy
Energized & healthy
Aligned

one thing I can do today to feel that way is...
Get out in nature and call my bff

I am grateful for...

1. *All the delicious groceries I bought yesterday.*
2. *My friends and family who are supporting me with love and compassion.*
3. *My hard work and determination with my new project.*

yesterday's wins:

1. *I prioritized 10 minutes of really good self care time.*
2. *I received unexpected financial abundance!*
3. *I crushed my presentation and felt really confident!*

I trust the Universe to bring in...

Super aligned opportunities that will help me get to the next level!

The perfect tools, and resources to help me finish my project.

today's to-do list:

- *Do laundry*
- *Call Carolina*
- *Walk the puppy*
- *Finish part 3 of work project*

date: _____

today's word/intention is...

_____

today I want to feel...

one thing I can do today to feel that way is...

I am grateful for...

1. _____
2. _____
3. _____

yesterday's wins:

1. _____
2. _____
3. _____

I trust the Universe to bring in...

today's to-do list:

_____   _____

_____   _____

_____   _____

_____   _____

_____   _____

date:

today's word/intention is...

today I want to feel...

one thing I can do today to feel that way is...

I am grateful for...

1.
2.
3.

yesterday's wins:

1.
2.
3.

I trust the Universe to bring in...

today's to-do list:

date:

today's word/intention is...

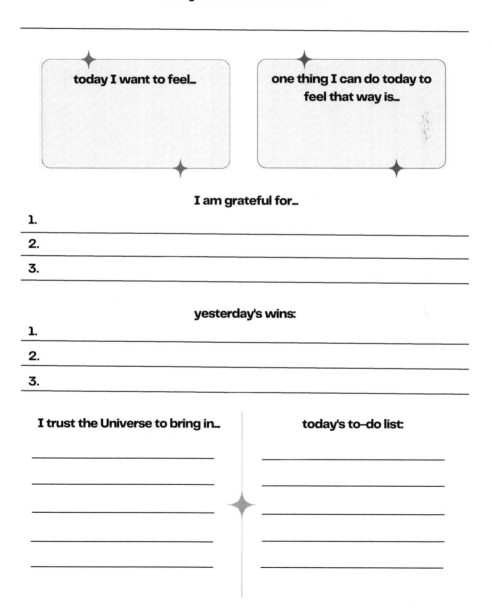

today I want to feel...

one thing I can do today to feel that way is...

I am grateful for...

1.
2.
3.

yesterday's wins:

1.
2.
3.

I trust the Universe to bring in...

today's to-do list:

date: _____

today's word/intention is...

_____

today I want to feel...	one thing I can do today to feel that way is...

I am grateful for...

1. _____
2. _____
3. _____

yesterday's wins:

1. _____
2. _____
3. _____

I trust the Universe to bring in...

_____
_____
_____
_____
_____

today's to-do list:

_____
_____
_____
_____
_____

date:

today's word/intention is...

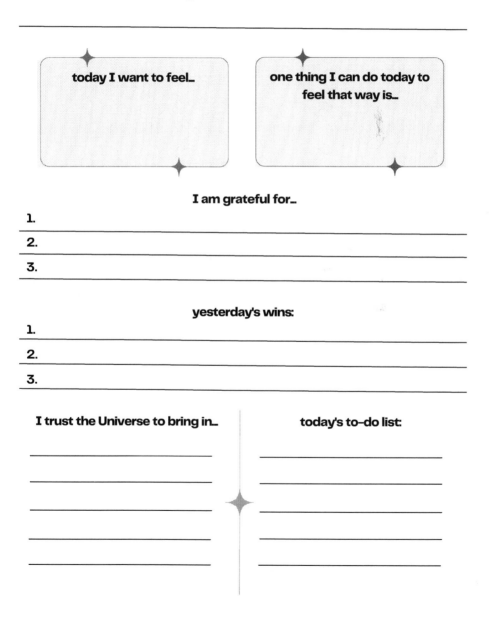

today I want to feel...

one thing I can do today to feel that way is...

I am grateful for...

1.
2.
3.

yesterday's wins:

1.
2.
3.

I trust the Universe to bring in...

today's to-do list:

date:

today's word/intention is...

today I want to feel...

one thing I can do today to feel that way is...

I am grateful for...

1.
2.
3.

yesterday's wins:

1.
2.
3.

I trust the Universe to bring in...

today's to-do list:

date: _____

today's word/intention is...

_____

today I want to feel...	one thing I can do today to feel that way is...

I am grateful for...

1. _____
2. _____
3. _____

yesterday's wins:

1. _____
2. _____
3. _____

I trust the Universe to bring in...

_____

_____

_____

_____

_____

today's to-do list:

_____

_____

_____

_____

_____

date: _____

today's word/intention is...

_____

today I want to feel...

one thing I can do today to feel that way is...

I am grateful for...

1. _____
2. _____
3. _____

yesterday's wins:

1. _____
2. _____
3. _____

I trust the Universe to bring in...

_____

_____

_____

_____

_____

today's to-do list:

_____

_____

_____

_____

_____

date:

today's word/intention is...

today I want to feel...

one thing I can do today to feel that way is...

I am grateful for...

1.
2.
3.

yesterday's wins:

1.
2.
3.

I trust the Universe to bring in...

today's to-do list:

date: _____

today's word/intention is...

_____

| today I want to feel... | one thing I can do today to feel that way is... |

I am grateful for...

1. _____
2. _____
3. _____

yesterday's wins:

1. _____
2. _____
3. _____

I trust the Universe to bring in...

_____

_____

_____

_____

_____

today's to-do list:

_____

_____

_____

_____

_____

date: _____

today's word/intention is_

_____

| today I want to feel_ | one thing I can do today to feel that way is_ |

I am grateful for_

1. _____
2. _____
3. _____

yesterday's wins:

1. _____
2. _____
3. _____

I trust the Universe to bring in_

_____

_____

_____

_____

_____

today's to-do list:

_____

_____

_____

_____

_____

date:

today's word/intention is...

today I want to feel...

one thing I can do today to feel that way is...

I am grateful for...

1.
2.
3.

yesterday's wins:

1.
2.
3.

I trust the Universe to bring in...

today's to-do list:

date: _____

today's word/intention is...

_____

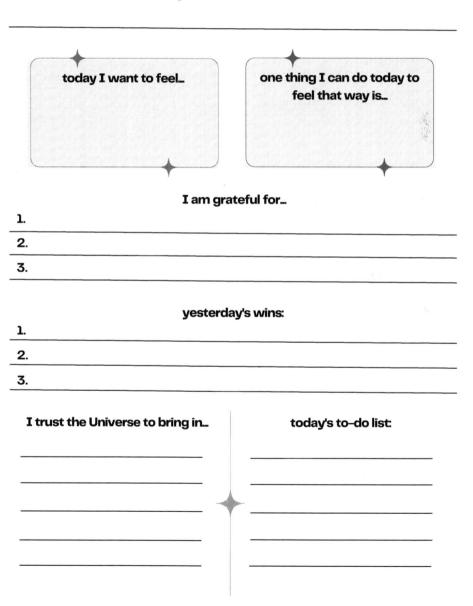

today I want to feel...

one thing I can do today to feel that way is...

I am grateful for...

1. _____
2. _____
3. _____

yesterday's wins:

1. _____
2. _____
3. _____

I trust the Universe to bring in...

today's to-do list:

_____   _____

_____   _____

_____   _____

_____   _____

_____   _____

date: _____

today's word/intention is...

_____

| today I want to feel... | one thing I can do today to feel that way is... |

I am grateful for...

1. _____
2. _____
3. _____

yesterday's wins:

1. _____
2. _____
3. _____

I trust the Universe to bring in...   **today's to–do list:**

_____   _____

_____   _____

_____   _____

_____   _____

_____   _____

date: _____

today's word/intention is...

_____

today I want to feel...

one thing I can do today to feel that way is...

I am grateful for...

1. _____
2. _____
3. _____

yesterday's wins:

1. _____
2. _____
3. _____

I trust the Universe to bring in...

_____
_____
_____
_____
_____

today's to-do list:

_____
_____
_____
_____
_____

date: _____

today's word/intention is...

_____

today I want to feel...	one thing I can do today to feel that way is...

I am grateful for...

1. _____
2. _____
3. _____

yesterday's wins:

1. _____
2. _____
3. _____

I trust the Universe to bring in...

_____

_____

_____

_____

_____

today's to-do list:

_____

_____

_____

_____

_____

date: _____

today's word/intention is...

_____

today I want to feel...	one thing I can do today to feel that way is...

I am grateful for...

1. _____
2. _____
3. _____

yesterday's wins:

1. _____
2. _____
3. _____

I trust the Universe to bring in...

_____

_____

_____

_____

_____

today's to-do list:

_____

_____

_____

_____

_____

date:

today's word/intention is...

today I want to feel...

one thing I can do today to feel that way is...

I am grateful for...

1.
2.
3.

yesterday's wins:

1.
2.
3.

I trust the Universe to bring in...

today's to-do list:

date: _____

> "Be faithful in small things because it is in them that your strength lies."
> – Mother Teresa

today's word/intention is...

_____

today I want to feel...	one thing I can do today to feel that way is...

I am grateful for...

1. _____
2. _____
3. _____

yesterday's wins:

1. _____
2. _____
3. _____

I trust the Universe to bring in...

_____

_____

_____

_____

_____

today's to-do list:

_____

_____

_____

_____

_____

date: _____

today's word/intention is...

_____

today I want to feel...

one thing I can do today to feel that way is...

I am grateful for...

1. _____
2. _____
3. _____

yesterday's wins:

1. _____
2. _____
3. _____

I trust the Universe to bring in...

_____
_____
_____
_____
_____

today's to-do list:

_____
_____
_____
_____
_____

date: _____

today's word/intention is...

_____

| today I want to feel... | one thing I can do today to feel that way is... |

I am grateful for...

1. _____
2. _____
3. _____

yesterday's wins:

1. _____
2. _____
3. _____

I trust the Universe to bring in...

_____

_____

_____

_____

_____

today's to-do list:

_____

_____

_____

_____

_____

date:

today's word/intention is...

today I want to feel...

one thing I can do today to feel that way is...

I am grateful for...

1.
2.
3.

yesterday's wins:

1.
2.
3.

I trust the Universe to bring in...

today's to-do list:

date: _____

today's word/intention is...

_____

today I want to feel...	one thing I can do today to feel that way is...

I am grateful for...

1. _____
2. _____
3. _____

yesterday's wins:

1. _____
2. _____
3. _____

I trust the Universe to bring in... | **today's to-do list:**

_____   _____

_____   _____

_____   _____

_____   _____

_____   _____

date: _____

today's word/intention is...

_____

today I want to feel...	one thing I can do today to feel that way is...

I am grateful for...

1. _____
2. _____
3. _____

yesterday's wins:

1. _____
2. _____
3. _____

I trust the Universe to bring in...

_____

_____

_____

_____

_____

today's to-do list:

_____

_____

_____

_____

_____

date: _____

today's word/intention is...

_____

today I want to feel...	one thing I can do today to feel that way is...

I am grateful for...

1. _____
2. _____
3. _____

yesterday's wins:

1. _____
2. _____
3. _____

I trust the Universe to bring in...

_____

_____

_____

_____

_____

today's to-do list:

_____

_____

_____

_____

_____

date: _____

today's word/intention is...

_____

| today I want to feel... | one thing I can do today to feel that way is... |

I am grateful for...

1. _____
2. _____
3. _____

yesterday's wins:

1. _____
2. _____
3. _____

I trust the Universe to bring in...

_____

_____

_____

_____

_____

today's to-do list:

_____

_____

_____

_____

_____

date:

today's word/intention is...

today I want to feel...

one thing I can do today to feel that way is...

I am grateful for...

1.
2.
3.

yesterday's wins:

1.
2.
3.

I trust the Universe to bring in...

today's to-do list:

date:

today's word/intention is...

today I want to feel...

one thing I can do today to feel that way is...

I am grateful for...

1.
2.
3.

yesterday's wins:

1.
2.
3.

I trust the Universe to bring in...

today's to-do list:

date: _____

today's word/intention is...

_____

today I want to feel...

one thing I can do today to feel that way is...

I am grateful for...

1. _____
2. _____
3. _____

yesterday's wins:

1. _____
2. _____
3. _____

I trust the Universe to bring in...

today's to-do list:

_____   _____

_____   _____

_____   _____

_____   _____

_____   _____

date: _____

today's word/intention is...

_____

| today I want to feel... | one thing I can do today to feel that way is... |

I am grateful for...

1. _____
2. _____
3. _____

yesterday's wins:

1. _____
2. _____
3. _____

I trust the Universe to bring in...

_____
_____
_____
_____
_____

today's to-do list:

_____
_____
_____
_____
_____

date: _____

today's word/intention is...

_____

| today I want to feel... | one thing I can do today to feel that way is... |

I am grateful for...

1. _____
2. _____
3. _____

yesterday's wins:

1. _____
2. _____
3. _____

I trust the Universe to bring in...   **today's to-do list:**

_____   _____

_____   _____

_____   _____

_____   _____

_____   _____

date: _____

today's word/intention is...

_____

| today I want to feel... | one thing I can do today to feel that way is... |

I am grateful for...

1. _____
2. _____
3. _____

yesterday's wins:

1. _____
2. _____
3. _____

I trust the Universe to bring in...   **today's to-do list:**

_____   _____

_____   _____

_____   _____

_____   _____

_____   _____

date:

today's word/intention is...

today I want to feel...

one thing I can do today to feel that way is...

I am grateful for...

1.
2.
3.

yesterday's wins:

1.
2.
3.

I trust the Universe to bring in...

today's to-do list:

date: _____

today's word/intention is...

_____

today I want to feel...	one thing I can do today to feel that way is...

I am grateful for...

1. _____
2. _____
3. _____

yesterday's wins:

1. _____
2. _____
3. _____

I trust the Universe to bring in...

_____

_____

_____

_____

_____

today's to-do list:

_____

_____

_____

_____

_____

date: _____

today's word/intention is...

_____

today I want to feel...	one thing I can do today to feel that way is...

I am grateful for...

1. _____
2. _____
3. _____

yesterday's wins:

1. _____
2. _____
3. _____

I trust the Universe to bring in...

_____

_____

_____

_____

_____

today's to-do list:

_____

_____

_____

_____

_____

date: _____

today's word/intention is...

_____

today I want to feel...

one thing I can do today to feel that way is...

I am grateful for...

1. _____
2. _____
3. _____

yesterday's wins:

1. _____
2. _____
3. _____

I trust the Universe to bring in...

today's to-do list:

_____   _____

_____   _____

_____   _____

_____   _____

_____   _____

date: _____

"Find out who you are and be that person. That's what your soul was put on this Earth to be. Find that truth, live that truth, and everything else will come."
– Ellen DeGeneres

today's word/intention is...

_____

today I want to feel...	one thing I can do today to feel that way is...

I am grateful for...

1. _____
2. _____
3. _____

yesterday's wins:

1. _____
2. _____
3. _____

I trust the Universe to bring in...

_____

_____

_____

_____

_____

today's to–do list:

_____

_____

_____

_____

_____

date: _____

> "Love yourself unconditionally, just as you love those closest
> to you despite their faults."
> – Les Brown

today's word/intention is...

_____

| today I want to feel... | one thing I can do today to feel that way is... |

I am grateful for...

1. _____
2. _____
3. _____

yesterday's wins:

1. _____
2. _____
3. _____

I trust the Universe to bring in...   **today's to-do list:**

_____   _____

_____   _____

_____   _____

_____   _____

_____   _____

date: _____

today's word/intention is...

_____

today I want to feel...	one thing I can do today to feel that way is...

I am grateful for...

1. _____
2. _____
3. _____

yesterday's wins:

1. _____
2. _____
3. _____

I trust the Universe to bring in...

_____
_____
_____
_____
_____

today's to-do list:

_____
_____
_____
_____
_____

date: _____

today's word/intention is...

_____

| today I want to feel... | one thing I can do today to feel that way is... |

I am grateful for...

1. _____
2. _____
3. _____

yesterday's wins:

1. _____
2. _____
3. _____

I trust the Universe to bring in...

_____

_____

_____

_____

_____

today's to-do list:

_____

_____

_____

_____

_____

date: _____

today's word/intention is_

_____

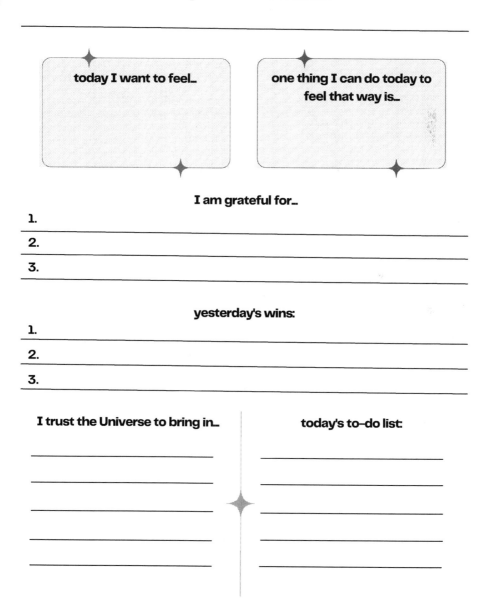

today I want to feel_

one thing I can do today to feel that way is_

I am grateful for_

1. _____
2. _____
3. _____

yesterday's wins:

1. _____
2. _____
3. _____

I trust the Universe to bring in_

today's to-do list:

date: _____

today's word/intention is...

_____

| today I want to feel... | one thing I can do today to feel that way is... |

I am grateful for...

1. _____
2. _____
3. _____

yesterday's wins:

1. _____
2. _____
3. _____

I trust the Universe to bring in... | **today's to–do list:**

_____ _____

_____ _____

_____ _____

_____ _____

_____ _____

date: _____

today's word/intention is...

_____

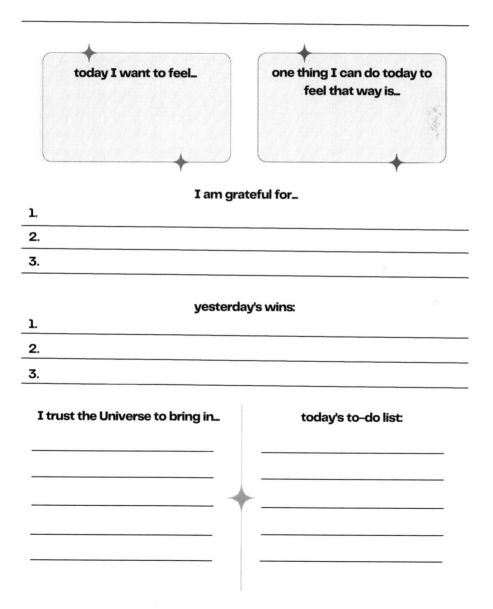

today I want to feel...

one thing I can do today to feel that way is...

I am grateful for...

1. _____
2. _____
3. _____

yesterday's wins:

1. _____
2. _____
3. _____

I trust the Universe to bring in...

today's to-do list:

date: _____

today's word/intention is_

_____

today I want to feel_	one thing I can do today to feel that way is_

I am grateful for_

1. _____
2. _____
3. _____

yesterday's wins:

1. _____
2. _____
3. _____

I trust the Universe to bring in_ | **today's to-do list:**

_____ | _____

_____ | _____

_____ | _____

_____ | _____

_____ | _____

date: _____

today's word/intention is...

_____

today I want to feel...

one thing I can do today to feel that way is...

I am grateful for...

1. _____
2. _____
3. _____

yesterday's wins:

1. _____
2. _____
3. _____

I trust the Universe to bring in...

today's to-do list:

date:

today's word/intention is...

today I want to feel...

one thing I can do today to
feel that way is...

I am grateful for...

1.
2.
3.

yesterday's wins:

1.
2.
3.

I trust the Universe to bring in...

today's to-do list:

date: _____

today's word/intention is...

_____

today I want to feel...	one thing I can do today to feel that way is...

I am grateful for...

1. _____
2. _____
3. _____

yesterday's wins:

1. _____
2. _____
3. _____

I trust the Universe to bring in...

_____

_____

_____

_____

_____

today's to-do list:

_____

_____

_____

_____

_____

date:

today's word/intention is...

| today I want to feel... | one thing I can do today to feel that way is... |

I am grateful for...

1.
2.
3.

yesterday's wins:

1.
2.
3.

I trust the Universe to bring in...

today's to-do list:

date: _____

today's word/intention is...

_____

today I want to feel...	one thing I can do today to feel that way is...

I am grateful for...

1. _____
2. _____
3. _____

yesterday's wins:

1. _____
2. _____
3. _____

I trust the Universe to bring in...   **today's to-do list:**

_____   _____

_____   _____

_____   _____

_____   _____

_____   _____

date: _____

today's word/intention is...

_____

today I want to feel...

one thing I can do today to feel that way is...

I am grateful for...

1. _____
2. _____
3. _____

yesterday's wins:

1. _____
2. _____
3. _____

I trust the Universe to bring in...

_____

_____

_____

_____

_____

today's to-do list:

_____

_____

_____

_____

_____

date:

today's word/intention is...

| today I want to feel... | one thing I can do today to feel that way is... |

I am grateful for...

1.
2.
3.

yesterday's wins:

1.
2.
3.

I trust the Universe to bring in...   **today's to-do list:**

date: _____

today's word/intention is...

_____

today I want to feel...

one thing I can do today to feel that way is...

I am grateful for...

1. _____
2. _____
3. _____

yesterday's wins:

1. _____
2. _____
3. _____

I trust the Universe to bring in...

today's to-do list:

_____   _____

_____   _____

_____   _____

_____   _____

_____   _____

date: _____

today's word/intention is__

_____

> today I want to feel__

> one thing I can do today to
> feel that way is__

I am grateful for__

1. _____
2. _____
3. _____

yesterday's wins:

1. _____
2. _____
3. _____

I trust the Universe to bring in__

_____

_____

_____

_____

_____

today's to–do list:

_____

_____

_____

_____

_____

date:

today's word/intention is...

today I want to feel...

one thing I can do today to feel that way is...

I am grateful for...

1.
2.
3.

yesterday's wins:

1.
2.
3.

I trust the Universe to bring in...

today's to-do list:

date:

today's word/intention is...

today I want to feel...

one thing I can do today to feel that way is...

I am grateful for...

1.
2.
3.

yesterday's wins:

1.
2.
3.

I trust the Universe to bring in...

today's to-do list:

date:

today's word/intention is...

today I want to feel...

one thing I can do today to feel that way is...

I am grateful for...

1.
2.
3.

yesterday's wins:

1.
2.
3.

I trust the Universe to bring in...

today's to–do list:

date: _____

today's word/intention is...

_____

today I want to feel...

one thing I can do today to feel that way is...

I am grateful for...

1. _____
2. _____
3. _____

yesterday's wins:

1. _____
2. _____
3. _____

I trust the Universe to bring in...

_____

_____

_____

_____

_____

today's to-do list:

_____

_____

_____

_____

_____

date: _____

today's word/intention is...

_____

| today I want to feel... | one thing I can do today to feel that way is... |

I am grateful for...

1. _____
2. _____
3. _____

yesterday's wins:

1. _____
2. _____
3. _____

I trust the Universe to bring in...	today's to-do list:
_____	_____
_____	_____
_____	_____
_____	_____
_____	_____

date: _____

today's word/intention is_

_____

today I want to feel_	one thing I can do today to feel that way is_

I am grateful for_

1. _____
2. _____
3. _____

yesterday's wins:

1. _____
2. _____
3. _____

I trust the Universe to bring in_

_____

_____

_____

_____

_____

today's to-do list:

_____

_____

_____

_____

_____

date: _____

> "No one saves us but ourselves. No one can and no one may.
> We ourselves must walk the path."
> – Buddha

today's word/intention is__

_____

today I want to feel__	one thing I can do today to feel that way is...

I am grateful for__

1. _____
2. _____
3. _____

yesterday's wins:

1. _____
2. _____
3. _____

I trust the Universe to bring in__

_____

_____

_____

_____

_____

today's to–do list:

_____

_____

_____

_____

_____

date: _____

today's word/intention is...

_____

today I want to feel...	one thing I can do today to feel that way is...

I am grateful for...

1. _____
2. _____
3. _____

yesterday's wins:

1. _____
2. _____
3. _____

I trust the Universe to bring in...

_____

_____

_____

_____

_____

today's to-do list:

_____

_____

_____

_____

_____

date:

today's word/intention is...

today I want to feel...

one thing I can do today to feel that way is...

I am grateful for...

1.
2.
3.

yesterday's wins:

1.
2.
3.

I trust the Universe to bring in...

today's to-do list:

date: _____

today's word/intention is...

_____

today I want to feel...	one thing I can do today to feel that way is...

I am grateful for...

1. _____
2. _____
3. _____

yesterday's wins:

1. _____
2. _____
3. _____

I trust the Universe to bring in...

_____

_____

_____

_____

_____

today's to-do list:

_____

_____

_____

_____

_____

date: _____

today's word/intention is...

_____

| today I want to feel... | one thing I can do today to feel that way is... |

I am grateful for...

1. _____
2. _____
3. _____

yesterday's wins:

1. _____
2. _____
3. _____

I trust the Universe to bring in...

_____
_____
_____
_____
_____

today's to-do list:

_____
_____
_____
_____
_____

date:

today's word/intention is...

today I want to feel...

one thing I can do today to feel that way is...

I am grateful for...

1.
2.
3.

yesterday's wins:

1.
2.
3.

I trust the Universe to bring in...

today's to-do list:

date: _____

today's word/intention is...

_____

| today I want to feel... | one thing I can do today to feel that way is... |

I am grateful for...

1. _____
2. _____
3. _____

yesterday's wins:

1. _____
2. _____
3. _____

I trust the Universe to bring in...

_____

_____

_____

_____

_____

today's to-do list:

_____

_____

_____

_____

_____

date: _____

today's word/intention is...

_____

today I want to feel...	one thing I can do today to feel that way is...

I am grateful for...

1. _____
2. _____
3. _____

yesterday's wins:

1. _____
2. _____
3. _____

I trust the Universe to bring in...

_____

_____

_____

_____

_____

today's to-do list:

_____

_____

_____

_____

_____

date: _____

today's word/intention is...

_____

today I want to feel...	one thing I can do today to feel that way is...

I am grateful for...

1. _____
2. _____
3. _____

yesterday's wins:

1. _____
2. _____
3. _____

I trust the Universe to bring in...	today's to-do list:
_____	_____
_____	_____
_____	_____
_____	_____
_____	_____

date: _____

today's word/intention is...

_____

today I want to feel...

one thing I can do today to feel that way is...

I am grateful for...

1. _____
2. _____
3. _____

yesterday's wins:

1. _____
2. _____
3. _____

I trust the Universe to bring in...

_____
_____
_____
_____
_____

today's to-do list:

_____
_____
_____
_____
_____

date: _____

> "When you are truly clear about what you want, the whole universe stands on tiptoe waiting to assist you in miraculous and amazing ways to manifest your dream or intention." - Constance Arnold

today's word/intention is...

_____

| today I want to feel... | one thing I can do today to feel that way is... |

I am grateful for...

1. _____
2. _____
3. _____

yesterday's wins:

1. _____
2. _____
3. _____

I trust the Universe to bring in...

_____

_____

_____

_____

_____

today's to-do list:

_____

_____

_____

_____

_____

date: _____

today's word/intention is...

_____

today I want to feel...	one thing I can do today to feel that way is...

I am grateful for...

1. _____
2. _____
3. _____

yesterday's wins:

1. _____
2. _____
3. _____

I trust the Universe to bring in...

_____

_____

_____

_____

_____

today's to-do list:

_____

_____

_____

_____

_____

date: _____

today's word/intention is...

_____

| today I want to feel... | one thing I can do today to feel that way is... |

I am grateful for...

1. _____
2. _____
3. _____

yesterday's wins:

1. _____
2. _____
3. _____

I trust the Universe to bring in...

_____

_____

_____

_____

_____

today's to-do list:

_____

_____

_____

_____

_____

date: _____

today's word/intention is...

_____

today I want to feel...	one thing I can do today to feel that way is...

I am grateful for...

1. _____
2. _____
3. _____

yesterday's wins:

1. _____
2. _____
3. _____

I trust the Universe to bring in...

_____

_____

_____

_____

_____

today's to-do list:

_____

_____

_____

_____

_____

date: _____

today's word/intention is...

_____

today I want to feel...	one thing I can do today to feel that way is...

I am grateful for...

1. _____
2. _____
3. _____

yesterday's wins:

1. _____
2. _____
3. _____

I trust the Universe to bring in...

_____

_____

_____

_____

_____

today's to-do list:

_____

_____

_____

_____

_____

date: _____

today's word/intention is...

_____

today I want to feel...	one thing I can do today to feel that way is...

I am grateful for...

1. _____
2. _____
3. _____

yesterday's wins:

1. _____
2. _____
3. _____

I trust the Universe to bring in...

_____
_____
_____
_____
_____

today's to-do list:

_____
_____
_____
_____
_____

date:

today's word/intention is...

today I want to feel...

one thing I can do today to feel that way is...

I am grateful for...

1.
2.
3.

yesterday's wins:

1.
2.
3.

I trust the Universe to bring in...

today's to-do list:

date:

today's word/intention is...

today I want to feel...

one thing I can do today to feel that way is...

I am grateful for...

1.
2.
3.

yesterday's wins:

1.
2.
3.

I trust the Universe to bring in...

today's to–do list:

date: _____

today's word/intention is...

_____

today I want to feel...	one thing I can do today to feel that way is...

I am grateful for...

1. _____
2. _____
3. _____

yesterday's wins:

1. _____
2. _____
3. _____

I trust the Universe to bring in...

_____

_____

_____

_____

_____

today's to-do list:

_____

_____

_____

_____

_____

date:

today's word/intention is...

today I want to feel...

one thing I can do today to feel that way is...

I am grateful for...

1.
2.
3.

yesterday's wins:

1.
2.
3.

I trust the Universe to bring in...

today's to-do list:

date: _____

today's word/intention is...

_____

| today I want to feel... | one thing I can do today to feel that way is... |

I am grateful for...

1. _____
2. _____
3. _____

yesterday's wins:

1. _____
2. _____
3. _____

I trust the Universe to bring in...

_____

_____

_____

_____

_____

today's to-do list:

_____

_____

_____

_____

_____

date: _____

today's word/intention is...

_____

today I want to feel...	one thing I can do today to feel that way is...

I am grateful for...

1. _____
2. _____
3. _____

yesterday's wins:

1. _____
2. _____
3. _____

I trust the Universe to bring in...

_____

_____

_____

_____

_____

today's to–do list:

_____

_____

_____

_____

_____

date: _____

today's word/intention is...

_____

today I want to feel...

one thing I can do today to feel that way is...

I am grateful for...

1. _____
2. _____
3. _____

yesterday's wins:

1. _____
2. _____
3. _____

I trust the Universe to bring in...

_____

_____

_____

_____

_____

today's to-do list:

_____

_____

_____

_____

_____

date:

today's word/intention is...

today I want to feel...

one thing I can do today to feel that way is...

I am grateful for...

1.
2.
3.

yesterday's wins:

1.
2.
3.

I trust the Universe to bring in...

today's to–do list:

date:

today's word/intention is...

today I want to feel...

one thing I can do today to
feel that way is...

I am grateful for...

1.
2.
3.

yesterday's wins:

1.
2.
3.

I trust the Universe to bring in...

today's to-do list:

date: _____

today's word/intention is...

_____

today I want to feel...

one thing I can do today to feel that way is...

I am grateful for...

1. _____
2. _____
3. _____

yesterday's wins:

1. _____
2. _____
3. _____

I trust the Universe to bring in...

_____

_____

_____

_____

_____

today's to-do list:

_____

_____

_____

_____

_____

date: _____

today's word/intention is...

_____

| today I want to feel... | one thing I can do today to feel that way is... |

I am grateful for...

1. _____
2. _____
3. _____

yesterday's wins:

1. _____
2. _____
3. _____

I trust the Universe to bring in...   **today's to-do list:**

_____   _____

_____   _____

_____   _____

_____   _____

_____   _____

date:

today's word/intention is...

today I want to feel...

one thing I can do today to feel that way is...

I am grateful for...

1.
2.
3.

yesterday's wins:

1.
2.
3.

I trust the Universe to bring in...

today's to-do list:

date: _____

today's word/intention is...

_____

today I want to feel...

one thing I can do today to feel that way is...

I am grateful for...

1. _____
2. _____
3. _____

yesterday's wins:

1. _____
2. _____
3. _____

I trust the Universe to bring in...

_____
_____
_____
_____
_____

today's to-do list:

_____
_____
_____
_____
_____

date: _____

today's word/intention is...

_____   _____

| today I want to feel... | one thing I can do today to feel that way is... |

I am grateful for...

1. _____
2. _____
3. _____

yesterday's wins:

1. _____
2. _____
3. _____

I trust the Universe to bring in...   **today's to-do list:**

_____   _____

_____   _____

_____   _____

_____   _____

_____   _____

date:

today's word/intention is...

today I want to feel...

one thing I can do today to feel that way is...

I am grateful for...

1.
2.
3.

yesterday's wins:

1.
2.
3.

I trust the Universe to bring in...

today's to-do list:

date: _____

today's word/intention is...

_____

today I want to feel...	one thing I can do today to feel that way is...

I am grateful for...

1. _____
2. _____
3. _____

yesterday's wins:

1. _____
2. _____
3. _____

I trust the Universe to bring in...

_____

_____

_____

_____

_____

today's to-do list:

_____

_____

_____

_____

_____

date:

today's word/intention is...

today I want to feel...

one thing I can do today to feel that way is...

I am grateful for...

1.
2.
3.

yesterday's wins:

1.
2.
3.

I trust the Universe to bring in...

today's to-do list:

date: _____

today's word/intention is...

_____

today I want to feel...	one thing I can do today to feel that way is...

I am grateful for...

1. _____
2. _____
3. _____

yesterday's wins:

1. _____
2. _____
3. _____

I trust the Universe to bring in...

_____

_____

_____

_____

_____

today's to-do list:

_____

_____

_____

_____

_____

date: _____

> "Joy is what happens to us when we allow ourselves
> to recognize how good things really are."
> — Marianne Williamson

today's word/intention is...

_____

today I want to feel...

one thing I can do today to feel that way is...

I am grateful for...

1. _____
2. _____
3. _____

yesterday's wins:

1. _____
2. _____
3. _____

I trust the Universe to bring in...

_____

_____

_____

_____

_____

today's to-do list:

_____

_____

_____

_____

_____

date:

today's word/intention is...

today I want to feel...

one thing I can do today to feel that way is...

I am grateful for...

1.
2.
3.

yesterday's wins:

1.
2.
3.

I trust the Universe to bring in...

today's to–do list:

date: _____

today's word/intention is...

_____

today I want to feel...	one thing I can do today to feel that way is...

I am grateful for...

1. _____
2. _____
3. _____

yesterday's wins:

1. _____
2. _____
3. _____

I trust the Universe to bring in...

_____

_____

_____

_____

_____

today's to-do list:

_____

_____

_____

_____

_____

date: _____

today's word/intention is...

_____

today I want to feel...	one thing I can do today to feel that way is...

I am grateful for...

1. _____
2. _____
3. _____

yesterday's wins:

1. _____
2. _____
3. _____

I trust the Universe to bring in...

_____

_____

_____

_____

_____

today's to–do list:

_____

_____

_____

_____

_____

date:

today's word/intention is...

today I want to feel...

one thing I can do today to feel that way is...

I am grateful for...

1.
2.
3.

yesterday's wins:

1.
2.
3.

I trust the Universe to bring in...

today's to-do list:

date: _____

today's word/intention is...

_____

today I want to feel...

one thing I can do today to feel that way is...

I am grateful for...

1. _____
2. _____
3. _____

yesterday's wins:

1. _____
2. _____
3. _____

I trust the Universe to bring in...

today's to-do list:

_____   _____

_____   _____

_____   _____

_____   _____

_____   _____

date:

today's word/intention is...

today I want to feel...

one thing I can do today to feel that way is...

I am grateful for...

1.
2.
3.

yesterday's wins:

1.
2.
3.

I trust the Universe to bring in...

today's to-do list:

date: _____

today's word/intention is...

_____

| today I want to feel... | one thing I can do today to feel that way is... |

I am grateful for...

1. _____
2. _____
3. _____

yesterday's wins:

1. _____
2. _____
3. _____

I trust the Universe to bring in...

_____

_____

_____

_____

_____

today's to-do list:

_____

_____

_____

_____

_____

date: _____

today's word/intention is...

_____

today I want to feel...	one thing I can do today to feel that way is...

I am grateful for...

1. _____
2. _____
3. _____

yesterday's wins:

1. _____
2. _____
3. _____

I trust the Universe to bring in...

_____

_____

_____

_____

_____

today's to-do list:

_____

_____

_____

_____

_____

date: _____

today's word/intention is...

_____

| today I want to feel... | one thing I can do today to feel that way is... |

I am grateful for...

1. _____
2. _____
3. _____

yesterday's wins:

1. _____
2. _____
3. _____

I trust the Universe to bring in...   **today's to-do list:**

_____   _____

_____   _____

_____   _____

_____   _____

_____   _____

date: _____

today's word/intention is...

_____

today I want to feel...

one thing I can do today to feel that way is...

I am grateful for...

1. _____
2. _____
3. _____

yesterday's wins:

1. _____
2. _____
3. _____

I trust the Universe to bring in...

_____
_____
_____
_____
_____

today's to-do list:

_____
_____
_____
_____
_____

date: _____

today's word/intention is...

_____

today I want to feel...

one thing I can do today to feel that way is...

I am grateful for...

1. _____
2. _____
3. _____

yesterday's wins:

1. _____
2. _____
3. _____

I trust the Universe to bring in...

_____

_____

_____

_____

_____

today's to-do list:

_____

_____

_____

_____

_____

date: _____

today's word/intention is...

_____

| today I want to feel... | one thing I can do today to feel that way is... |

I am grateful for...

1. _____
2. _____
3. _____

yesterday's wins:

1. _____
2. _____
3. _____

I trust the Universe to bring in...

_____

_____

_____

_____

_____

today's to-do list:

_____

_____

_____

_____

_____

date:

today's word/intention is...

today I want to feel...

one thing I can do today to feel that way is...

I am grateful for...

1.
2.
3.

yesterday's wins:

1.
2.
3.

I trust the Universe to bring in...

today's to-do list:

date:

today's word/intention is...

today I want to feel...

one thing I can do today to feel that way is...

I am grateful for...

1.
2.
3.

yesterday's wins:

1.
2.
3.

I trust the Universe to bring in...

today's to-do list:

date: _____

today's word/intention is...

_____

| today I want to feel... | one thing I can do today to feel that way is... |

I am grateful for...

1. _____
2. _____
3. _____

yesterday's wins:

1. _____
2. _____
3. _____

I trust the Universe to bring in...   **today's to-do list:**

_____   _____

_____   _____

_____   _____

_____   _____

_____   _____

date:

today's word/intention is...

today I want to feel...

one thing I can do today to feel that way is...

I am grateful for...

1.
2.
3.

yesterday's wins:

1.
2.
3.

I trust the Universe to bring in...

_____

_____

_____

_____

_____

today's to-do list:

_____

_____

_____

_____

_____

date: _____

today's word/intention is...

_____

today I want to feel...	one thing I can do today to feel that way is...

I am grateful for...

1. _____
2. _____
3. _____

yesterday's wins:

1. _____
2. _____
3. _____

I trust the Universe to bring in...

_____

_____

_____

_____

_____

today's to-do list:

_____

_____

_____

_____

_____

date: _____

today's word/intention is...

_____

today I want to feel...	one thing I can do today to feel that way is...

I am grateful for...

1. _____
2. _____
3. _____

yesterday's wins:

1. _____
2. _____
3. _____

I trust the Universe to bring in...　　　　**today's to-do list:**

_____　　　_____

_____　　　_____

_____　　　_____

_____　　　_____

_____　　　_____

date: _____

today's word/intention is...

_____

today I want to feel...	one thing I can do today to feel that way is...

I am grateful for...

1. _____
2. _____
3. _____

yesterday's wins:

1. _____
2. _____
3. _____

I trust the Universe to bring in...

_____
_____
_____
_____
_____

today's to-do list:

_____
_____
_____
_____
_____

date: _____

today's word/intention is...

_____

| today I want to feel... | one thing I can do today to feel that way is... |

I am grateful for...

1. _____
2. _____
3. _____

yesterday's wins:

1. _____
2. _____
3. _____

I trust the Universe to bring in...

_____

_____

_____

_____

_____

today's to-do list:

_____

_____

_____

_____

_____

date: _____

today's word/intention is...

_____

today I want to feel...	one thing I can do today to feel that way is...

I am grateful for...

1. _____
2. _____
3. _____

yesterday's wins:

1. _____
2. _____
3. _____

I trust the Universe to bring in...

_____

_____

_____

_____

_____

today's to-do list:

_____

_____

_____

_____

_____

date: _____

today's word/intention is...

_____

today I want to feel...	one thing I can do today to feel that way is...

I am grateful for...

1. _____
2. _____
3. _____

yesterday's wins:

1. _____
2. _____
3. _____

I trust the Universe to bring in...

_____

_____

_____

_____

_____

today's to-do list:

_____

_____

_____

_____

_____

date: _____

"If you change the way you look at things, the things you look at change"
— Dr. Wayne Dyer

today's word/intention is...

_____

| today I want to feel... | one thing I can do today to feel that way is... |

I am grateful for...

1. _____
2. _____
3. _____

yesterday's wins:

1. _____
2. _____
3. _____

I trust the Universe to bring in...

_____

_____

_____

_____

_____

today's to-do list:

_____

_____

_____

_____

_____

date: _____

today's word/intention is...

_____

today I want to feel...	one thing I can do today to feel that way is...

I am grateful for...

1. _____
2. _____
3. _____

yesterday's wins:

1. _____
2. _____
3. _____

I trust the Universe to bring in...

_____

_____

_____

_____

_____

today's to-do list:

_____

_____

_____

_____

_____

date: _____

today's word/intention is...

_____

today I want to feel...	one thing I can do today to feel that way is...

I am grateful for...

1. _____
2. _____
3. _____

yesterday's wins:

1. _____
2. _____
3. _____

I trust the Universe to bring in... | **today's to-do list:**

_____ | _____

_____ | _____

_____ | _____

_____ | _____

_____ | _____

date:

today's word/intention is...

today I want to feel...

one thing I can do today to feel that way is...

I am grateful for...

1.
2.
3.

yesterday's wins:

1.
2.
3.

I trust the Universe to bring in...

today's to-do list:

Made in United States
Orlando, FL
24 July 2022

20124528R00070